GIVE
everything

a quote book for dreamers
by gloria marie pelcher

Copyright © 2013 Gloria Marie Pelcher

All rights reserved. No portion of this book may be used or reproduced in any manner whatsoever without written permission of the author or Creative Bluebird except in the case of brief quotations embodied in critical articles and reviews.

GIVE everything

ISBN-13: 978-0615803647 (Creative Bluebird)

ISBN-10: 0615803644

Creative Bluebird
www.creativebluebird.com

Cover Design: GLORIA MARIE PELCHER

based on artwork by Marish

For book inquiries please visit
creativebluebird.com/contact

For my family…like before!

CONTENTS

INTRODUCTION	1
DREAM	2
LIVE	26
WORK	94
LOVE	125
MY FAVORITE QUOTE	144

INTRODUCTION

A good quote will challenge the way you think, a set of thought provoking words that could possibly change your whole life.

Most of the quotes in this book come from a collection of quotes I've been collecting since the 90's! Over the years these quotes have inspired me to chase down dreams and conquer mountains. My favorite quote is by Abraham Lincoln, "I will prepare, and someday my chance will come."

I have divided the quotes in this book into four sections of DREAM, LIVE, WORK, and LOVE. Success is a balance! I hope this collection of quotes help you dream incredible dreams, live an awesome life, find and do worthwhile work, and above all love!

Gloria Marie Pelcher

DREAM

To be a dreamer in a world of naysayers is a hard thing to be. Most people only do things that have been done before, they never stretch their imagination to what could be. But what if you did?

everything

There's only one way to succeed in anything and that is to give everything. I do and I demand that my players do. Any man's finest hour is when he has worked his heart out in a good cause and lies exhausted on the field of battle…victorious.

Vince Lombardi

GIVE

Do not let what you cannot do interfere with what you can do.

                                    John Wooden

everything

We are the music-makers, and we are the Dreamers of Dreams.

Willy Wonka

GIVE

Progress always involves risk; you can't steal second base and keep your foot on first.
Frederick Wilcox

everything

Obstacles are those frightful things you see when you take your eyes off your goal.
Henry Ford

GIVE

If one dream should fall and break into a thousand pieces, never be afraid to pick one of those pieces up and begin again.

Flavia Weedn

everything

It's not what you are that holds you back, it's what you think you're not.

Denis Waitley

GIVE

You never really lose until you quit trying.

Mike Ditka

everything

Courage is fear that has said its prayers.

Dorothy Bernard

GIVE

I wasn't going to be one of those people who died wondering what if? I would keep putting my dreams to the test - even though it meant living with uncertainty and fear of failure. This is the shadowland of hope, and anyone with a dream must learn to live there.

Alex Haley

everything

Dream as if you'll live forever. Live as if you'll die tomorrow.

James Dean

Whatever you do, or dream you can, begin it. Boldness has genius and power and magic in it.

Johann Wolfgang von Goethe

everything

You cannot discover new oceans, unless you have the courage to lose sight of the shore.

Andre Gide

GIVE

A head full of fears has no space for dreams.

Author Unknown

everything

And the trouble is, if you don't risk anything, you risk even more.

Erica Jong

GIVE

A #2 pencil and a dream can take you anywhere.

Joyce A. Myers

everything

Only you can hold yourself back, only you can stand in your own way, only you can help yourself.

Mikhail Strabo

GIVE

Just go out there and do what you've got to do.

Martina Navratilo

everything

Never give up on a dream just because of the time it will take to accomplish it. The time will pass anyway.
                              Earl Nightingale

GIVE

Doing new and different things doesn't always work, but if you don't try, you'll never do anything in a big way.

Jean Feiwel

everything

Walk with the dreamers, the believers, the courageous, the cheerful, the planners, the doers, the successful people with their heads in the clouds and their feet on the ground. Let their spirit ignite a fire within you to leave this world better than when you found it…
Wilferd Peterson

GIVE

The future belongs to those who believe in the beauty of their dreams.

Eleanor Roosevelt

everything

Sometimes all you need is 20 seconds of insane courage, and I promise you something great will come of it.

Benjamin Mee

LIVE

Sometimes it's hard to live, to speak, to give, to love, to be. There are many competing forces in the world, pulling you here and there. Breathe. Just breathe. That's life existing within you, and every little thing is going to be alright

everything

Life is either a daring adventure or nothing.

Helen Keller

GIVE

What does your anxiety do? It does not empty tomorrow of its sorrow, but it empties today of its strength.

Dr. Raymond Cramer

everything

Be yourself; everyone else is already taken.

Oscar Wilde

GIVE

In the end we will conserve only what we love; we will love only what we understand; and we will understand only what we are taught.

Baba Dioum

everything

Be who you are and say what you feel because those who mind don't matter and those who matter don't mind.

Dr. Suess

The greatest mistake you can make in life is to be continually fearing you will make one.

Elbert Hubbard

everything

Injustice anywhere is a threat to justice everywhere.
Martin Luther King Jr.

GIVE

The only people for me are the mad ones, the ones who are mad to live, mad to talk, mad to be saved, desirous of everything at the same time, the ones who never yawn or say a commonplace thing, but burn, burn, burn, like fabulous yellow roman candles exploding like spiders across the stars.

Jack Kerouac

everything

Enjoy life. This is not a dress rehearsal.

Author Unknown

GIVE

Whenever you fall, pick something up.

Oswald Avery

everything

Forgive them, even if they are not sorry.

Julian Casablancas

GIVE

Always be a first rate version of yourself and not a second rate version of someone else.
Judy Garland

everything

No man in the world has more courage than the man who can stop after eating one peanut.

Channing Pollock

GIVE

"How does one become a butterfly?" she asked pensively. "You must want to fly so much that you are willing to give up being a caterpillar."

Trina Paulus

everything

For a long time it seemed to me that life was about to begin - real life. But there was always something to be gotten through first, some unfinished business, time still to be served, a debt to be paid. At last it dawned on me that these obstacles were my life. This perspective has helped me to see there is no way to happiness. Happiness is the way. So treasure every moment you have and remember that time waits for no one. Happiness is a journey, not a destination...
Souza

If you want to stand out, don't be different, be outstanding.

Meredith West

everything

You are a living magnet. What you attract into your life is in harmony with your dominant thoughts.

Brian Tracy

GIVE

Most folks are about as happy as they make up their minds to be.

Abraham Lincoln

everything

If you want to make God laugh, tell him about your plans.

Woody Allen

Is he alone who has courage on his right hand and faith on his left hand?

Charles A. Lindbergh

everything

Dreams are illustrations from the book your soul is writing about yourself.

Marsha Norman

GIVE

Courage brother, do not stumble, though thy path be dark as night: There is a star to guide the humble, Trust in God, and do the right. Let the road be dark and dreary and its end far out of sight. Face it bravely, strong or weary. Trust in God, and do the right.

Norman Macleod

everything

Technology...the knack of arranging the world so that we don't have to experience it.

Max Frisch

GIVE

Every thought is a seed. If you plant crab apples, don't count on harvesting Golden Delicious.

Bill Meyer

everything

Universities are full of knowledge; the freshman bring a little in, the seniors take none away, and the knowledge there accumulates.

Abbott Lawrence Lowell

GIVE

Those who know others are intelligent
Those who know themselves have insight.
Those who master others have force
Those who master themselves have strength.

Those who know what is enough are wealthy.
Those who persevere have direction.
Those who maintain their position endure.
And those who die and yet do not perish,
    live on.

Lao Tzu

everything

The happiness of your life depends upon the quality of your thoughts: therefore, guard accordingly, and take care that you entertain no notions unsuitable to virtue and reasonable nature.

Marcus Aurelius

GIVE

So live that you wouldn't be ashamed to sell the family parrot to the town gossip.
Will Rogers

everything

Whoever fights monsters should see to it that in the process he does not become a monster. And if you gaze long enough into an abyss, the abyss will gaze back into you.

Friedrich Nietzsche

GIVE

Fate chooses our relatives, we choose our friends.

Jacques Delille

everything

If you realized how powerful your thoughts are, you would never think a negative thought.

Peace Pilgrim

GIVE

As scarce as truth is, the supply has always been in excess of the demand.

Josh Billings

everything

For attractive lips, speak words of kindness.
For lovely eyes, seek out the good in people.
For a slim figure, share your food with the hungry.
For beautiful hair, let a child run his or her fingers through it once a day.

Sam Levenson

GIVE

Sometimes I do get to places just when God is ready to have somebody click the shutter.

Ansel Adams

everything

I am strong because I believe in myself. I know who I am and what I can do. It doesn't matter what I look like, where I live, or who my friends are. What matters is the confidence that I carry within.

Reebok

GIVE

Do what you feel in your heart to be right – for you'll be criticized anyway.
Eleanor Roosevelt

everything

Life is a great big canvas, and you should throw all the paint on it you can.

Danny Kaye

GIVE

Although the world is full of suffering, it is also full of the overcoming of it.

Helen Keller

everything

It is not happy people who are thankful. It is thankful people who are happy.
Author Unknown

GIVE

We are the hero of our own story.

Mary McCarthy

everything

Our deepest fear is not that we are inadequate. Our deepest fear is that we are powerful beyond measure. It is our light, not our darkness that most frightens us. We ask ourselves, Who am I to be brilliant, gorgeous, talented, fabulous? Actually, who are you not to be? You are a child of God. Your playing small does not serve the world. There is nothing enlightened about shrinking so that other people won't feel insecure around you. We are all meant to shine, as children do. We were born to make manifest the glory of God that is within us. It's not just in some of us; it's in everyone. And as we let our own light shine, we unconsciously give other people permission to do the same. As we are liberated from our own fear, our presence automatically liberates others.

Marianne Williamson

GIVE

In three words I can sum up everything I've learned about life: It goes on.

Robert Frost

everything

If you have to ask whether or not you offended someone, you probably did. Apologizing only confirms it.

Space Ghost

GIVE

It's never too late, in fiction or in life, to revise.
                                                  Nancy Thayer

everything

Be strong when you are weak, brave when you are scared, and humble when you are victorious.

Author Unknown

What can you say about a society that says that God is dead and Elvis is alive.

Irv Kupcinet

everything

The only man who behaved sensibly was my tailor; he took my measurements anew every time he saw me, while all the rest went on with their old measurements and expected them to fit me.

George Bernard Shaw

GIVE

The young do not know enough to be prudent, and therefore they attempt the impossible - and achieve it, generation after generation.
Tom Clancy

everything

Never tell a young person that anything cannot be done. God may have been waiting centuries for someone ignorant enough of the impossible to do that very thing.

John Andrew Holmes

GIVE

Yesterday is a cancelled check; tomorrow is a promissory note; today is the only cash you have – so spend it wisely.

Kay Lyons

everything

If you can teach me not to think then you can teach me not to feel.

Shakespeare

GIVE

Hating people is like burning down your house to kill a rat.
Henry Emerson Fosdick

everything

Success is that old A B C – ability, breaks and courage.
Charles Luckman

GIVE

Change your thoughts and
you change your world.
                    Norman Vincent Peale

everything

Life is an opportunity, benefit from it.
Life is beauty, admire it.
Life is a dream, realize it.
Life is a challenge, meet it.
Life is a duty, complete it.
Life is a game, play it.
Life is a promise, fulfill it.
Life is sorrow, overcome it.
Life is a song, sing it.
Life is a struggle, accept it.
Life is a tragedy, confront it.
Life is an adventure, dare it.
Life is luck, make it.
Life is too precious, do not destroy it.
Life is life, fight for it.

Mother Teresa

GIVE

There is a gigantic difference between earning a great deal of money and being rich.
Marlene Dietrich

everything

It's better to make bold choices in life, than no choices at all or even mild choices.

Tim Allen

GIVE

Expecting life to treat you fairly because you're a good person is like expecting an angry bull not to charge because you're a vegetarian.

Shari R. Barr

everything

Take the first step in faith, you don't have to see the whole staircase, just take the first step.

Martin Luther King, Jr.

GIVE

"Come to the edge," He said;
"We are afraid," they said.
"Come to the edge," He said;
They came. He pushed them.
And they flew.

Guillaume Appolinaire

everything

You have brains in your head. Your feet in your shoes. You can steer yourself in any direction you choose.

Dr. Seuss

GIVE

Marvel not, my brethren, if the world hate you.

I John 3:13

everything

We must be the change we wish to see in the world.
Gandhi

GIVE

There aren't any great men. There are just great challenges that ordinary men like you and me are forced by circumstances to meet.

William F. Halsey

everything

The value of an idea has nothing whatsoever to do with the sincerity of the man who expresses it.

Oscar Wilde

GIVE

You've failed many times, although you may not remember. You fell down the first time you tried to walk. You almost drowned the first time you tried to swim, didn't you? Did you hit the ball the first time you swung a bat? Heavy hitters, the ones who hit the most home runs, also strike out a lot. R.H. Macy failed 7 times before his store in New York caught on. English novelist John Creasy got 753 rejection slips before he published 564 books. Babe Ruth struck out 1,330 times, but he also hit 714 home runs. Don't worry about failure. Worry about the chances you miss when you don't even try.

United Technologies

everything

If a train doesn't stop at your station, then it's not your train.

Marianne Williamson

GIVE

WORK

We are all talented, but it is work that separates us from each other. How bad do you want your dreams to come true? Be willing to be completely dedicated to your life's work.

everything

I will prepare, and someday my chance will come.
Abraham Lincoln

GIVE

We've heard that a million monkeys at a million keyboards could produce the Complete Works of Shakespeare; now, thanks to the Internet, we know this is not true.

Robert Wilensky

everything

The reason why worry kills more people than work is that more people worry than work.

Robert Frost

The principle is competing against yourself. It's about self-improvement, about being better than you were the day before.

Steve Young

everything

It's enough for you to do it once for a few men to remember you. But if you do it year after year, then many people remember you and they tell it to their children, and their children and grandchildren remember and, if it concerns books, they can read them. And if it's good enough, it will last as long as there are human beings.

Ernest Hemingway

GIVE

You have to learn the rules of the game. And then you have to play better than anyone else.

Dianne Feinstein

everything

A year from now you may wish you had started today.
Karen Lamb

GIVE

We must do our work for its own sake, not for fortune or attention or applause.
Steven Pressfield

everything

The greatest things ever done on Earth have been done little by little.
William Jennings Bryan

When you know what you want, and want it bad enough, you will find a way to get it.

Jim Rohn

everything

A disciplined mind leads to happiness, and an undisciplined mind leads to suffering.

Dalai Lama XIV

GIVE

Here is a test to find whether your mission on earth is finished: If you're alive, it isn't.

Richard Bach

everything

When you walk with purpose you collide with destiny.
Beatrice Berry

GIVE

When you want something, all the universe conspires in helping you to achieve it.
Paulo Coelho

everything

I do the very best I know how – the very best I can; and I mean to keep on doing so until the end.

Abraham Lincoln

GIVE

I cannot give you the formula for success, but I can give you the formula for failure, which is – try to please everybody.

Herbert Bayard Swope

everything

The key to motivation is to look at how far I have come rather than how far I have to go.

Hugh Prather

GIVE

I haven't failed. I have successfully discovered 12,000 ideas that don't work.

Thomas Edison

everything

Many of us spend half our time wishing for things we could have if we didn't spend half our time wishing.

Alexander Woollcott

GIVE

Success is liking yourself, liking what you do, and liking how you do it.

Maya Angelou

everything

If you always do what you always did, you'll always get what you always got.

Author Unknown

GIVE

Start where you are. Use what you have. Do what you can.

Arthur Ashe

everything

I don't try to work every day. I do work every day.

Beatrice Wood

Nothing in the world can take the place of persistence. Talent will not; nothing is more common than unsuccessful men with talent. Genius will not; unrewarded genius is almost a proverb. Education will not; the world is full of educated derelicts. Persistence and determination alone are omnipotent. The slogan "Press on" has solved and always will solve the problems of the human race.

Calvin Coolidge

everything

The one who removes a mountain begins by carrying away small stones.

Chinese Proverb

I've learned that there is no elevator to success. You have to take the stairs.

Author Unknown

everything

Luck is what happens when preparation meets opportunity.

Seneca

GIVE

If a thing is worth doing, it is worth doing well. If it is worth having, it is worth waiting for. If it is worth attaining, it is worth fighting for. If it is worth experiencing, it is worth putting aside time for.

Susan Jeffries

everything

Work harder than you think you possibly can.

Ben Affleck

GIVE

Do one thing every day that scares you.

Eleanor Roosevelt

everything

LOVE

Operate within love in all that you do. It is not the easiest thing to do but it is worth it time and time again. Make the decision to be intentional with love.

Keep love in your heart. A life without it is like a sunless garden when the flowers are dead.

Oscar Wilde

everything

I have decided to stick with love. Hate is too great a burden to bear.

Martin Luther King, Jr.

GIVE

Love does not begin and end the way we seem to think it does. Love is a battle, love is a war; love is a growing up.
James A. Baldwin

everything

Love begins at home, and it is not how much we do...but how much love we put in that action.

Mother Teresa

GIVE

If you live to be a hundred, I want to live to be a hundred minus one day so I never have to live without you.

A. A. Milne

everything

Love is life. And if you miss love, you miss life.

Leo Buscaglia

GIVE

The best thing to hold onto in life is each other.

Audrey Hepburn

everything

We love life, not because we are used to living but because we are used to loving.
Friedrich Nietzsche

GIVE

I can live without money, but I cannot live without love.
Judy Garland

everything

We waste time looking for the perfect lover, instead of creating the perfect love.
Tom Robbins

Charity suffereth long, and is kind; charity envieth not; charity vaunteth not itself, is not puffed up, Doth not behave itself unseemly, seeketh not her own, is not easily provoked, thinketh no evil; Rejoiceth not in iniquity, but rejoiceth in the truth; Beareth all things, believeth all things, hopeth all things, endureth all things. Charity never faileth: but whether there be prophecies, they shall fail; whether there be tongues, they shall cease; whether there be knowledge, it shall vanish away.

1 Corinthians 13:4-8

everything

Love is an irresistible desire to be irresistibly desired.
Robert Frost

GIVE

You know you're in love when you can't fall asleep because reality is finally better than your dreams.

Dr. Seuss

everything

We accept the love we think we deserve.

Stephen Chbosky

GIVE

If you judge people, you have no time to love them.

Mother Teresa

everything

I love you without knowing how, or when, or from where. I love you simply, without problems or pride: I love you in this way because I do not know any other way of loving but this, in which there is no I or you, so intimate that your hand upon my chest is my hand, so intimate that when I fall asleep your eyes close.

Pablo Neruda

GIVE

If I had a flower for every time I thought of you...I could walk through my garden forever.

Alfred Tennyson

everything

Most of all, let love guide your life.

Col. 3:14

My Favorite Quote

everything

ABOUT

gloria marie pelcher

GLORIA MARIE PELCHER lives in Dallas, TX. and is a writer, photographer, speaker, publisher, and owner of Creative Bluebird. She blogs regularly at gloriamarie.com and is committed to encouraging people to HAVE CRAZY FAITH!

Also by
GLORIA MARIE PELCHER

30 Things I Know For Certain
A Guide To Doing Incredible Things With Your Life
365 Affirmations
Keep Calm and Teach On

CONNECT :)

gm@gloriamarie.com
gloriamarie.com/subscribe
goodreads.com/gloriamarie
facebook.com/gloriamarie
twitter.com/gloriamarie
pinterest.com/gloriamarie
amazon.com/author/gloriamarie

Are you willing to give everything for your dreams? Join the conversation!

#giveeverything

everything

 **DREAM ON…**

www.ingramcontent.com/pod-product-compliance
Lightning Source LLC
Chambersburg PA
CBHW060759050426
42449CB00008B/1453